HOW TO UNF*CK

- YOUR -

FINANCES

A Little Bit Each Day

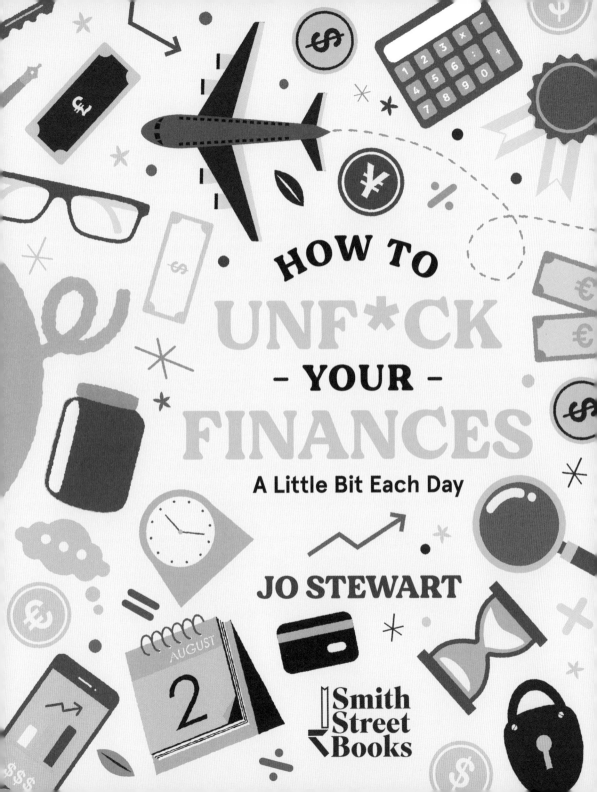

HOW TO
UNF*CK
- YOUR -
FINANCES

A Little Bit Each Day

JO STEWART

Smith Street Books

Contents

SPENDING
HOW TO UNF*CK YOUR FINANCES
53–71

DEBT BUSTING
HOW TO UNF*CK YOUR FINANCES
72–77

LIVING
HOW TO UNF*CK YOUR FINANCES
78–107

They say that money can't buy happiness, but anyone who believes that adage hasn't endured the sleepless nights that come with not being able to pay your bills.

The sense of freedom, peace, protection, and empowerment that comes with being financially secure is priceless, especially if you've started in struggle town.

It's important to remember that no matter where you've come from or what you're currently earning, achieving a fiscal glow up is possible. Will it be easy? Not at first. Will it be worth it? You better believe it.

While you probably weren't taught about money management in school, it's never too late to learn. Whether you're a student living on a shoestring budget, a freelancer following your dreams, or a corporate lawyer killing it in your first year at a big firm, managing your money is one of the most important skills you'll ever master.

It may feel like the deck has been stacked against you since birth. Seeing the rise of financial inequality sure can be disheartening. How can billionaires go to space when homelessness is still a thing? While we may not be able to change the obscene economic model we're a part of, we can change the way we go about our business.

Hopefully this book will motivate you to sort your finances out so that you can live a kickass life. Sure, some concepts may not be right for you (investing is near impossible if you're struggling to pay your rent) but hopefully the ideas in this book will kickstart your journey to financial freedom and help you unf*ck your finances for good.

SILO YOUR SAVINGS

Instead of keeping all your money in one bank account that you use for everything, try setting up sub accounts to keep yourself, well, accountable. Whether you're saving for an overseas trip or dream car, clearly defined sub accounts can help you reach your savings goals faster. Funneling your money into sub accounts for specific big-ticket buys or dream-fulfilling projects helps to keep your savings on track, because you know that money is for your trip to Paris, not $15 smoothies and all those other things you can't remember spending your money on.

SAVING

HOW TO UNF*CK YOUR FINANCES

BUILD AN EMERGENCY FUND

Cars break down, jobs can be lost, and dogs need to visit a vet when they locate and destroy your chocolate stash. Life emergencies will crop up, but how are you placed to pay for them? Having a healthy emergency fund to cover these situations is essential to your financial and emotional health. With a solid emergency fund in your arsenal, you'll be able to avoid costly high-interest credit card debt and even worse, predatory payday loans. The peace of mind that comes with having a financial buffer to cover unforeseen events is priceless. So give yourself some breathing space by building a fund to cushion yourself from life's blows. And nope, a trip to Coachella doesn't quality as an emergency.

BREAK IN AN EMERGENCY

SET IT TO AUTOPILOT

If you're a reluctant saver who can't seem to get it together, then automating your savings will remove the temptation to spend whatever money is in your account. If you get to the end of the month and have little money left, then automating the process will ensure you're saving, without even noticing it.

By setting up an automatic transfer to happen on every payday, you're essentially tricking yourself into saving. Whether you start small by saving $20 from each pay cycle or decide to sock away hundreds, the best part of this set-and-forget strategy is that once you set up a recurring transfer, you don't even need to remember to save – it magically happens without any effort or thought. With the funds stashed in a savings account, you'll be less likely to impulse-buy non-essentials like eye-wateringly expensive, hand-poured artisan candles that smell like heaven but send your bank balance straight to hell.

PUT WINDFALLS TO WORK

From getting a bonus at work, to receiving a juicy tax return, or finding a crisp $50 bill on the street – sometimes, the wheel of fortune spins in your favor. Instead of treating yourself immediately, consider treating your future self by saving that windfall. As money you weren't counting on receiving, surprise bonuses are super easy to blow on fun extras like a session at your favorite cocktail bar. Instead of giving your future (broke) self a hangover, stash that money in your savings account and watch it grow into a healthy nest egg.

HOW TO UNF*CK YOUR FINANCES · SAVING

STASH YOUR CASH

The humble piggy bank is an under-appreciated tool for saving money. Generations of children were taught how to save by slotting spare change into piggy banks or coin jars, and there's no reason why this practice can't continue into adulthood. If you feel your purse or wallet weighing you down, relieve the pressure by offloading all that excess metal into a coin jar. Get into the habit of not keeping coins on you at all by diverting all coins into your jar at home. You'll be surprised how quickly they all add up! Feeling flush? Throw some notes in there too. If you're prone to raiding your coin jar in moments of weakness, then guilt yourself by labeling it with your savings goal. Because nothing will stop you in your tracks more than the words "Gran's Birthday Gift Fund".

SAVING · HOW TO UNF*CK YOUR FINANCES

ROUND IT UP

Automatic savings apps are a pain-free way to save money here and there without noticing. Apps such as Acorns link to your bank account, round-up every purchase and stash away the extra dollars or cents in a separate investment account. Many banks have similar savings programs that allow customers to opt-in to programs that round-up purchases. Fifty cents here or there might not sound like much, but over time, it all adds up. Many of these apps have added features like bonus dollars for referring friends too. Of course, before signing up, check that the fees and conditions are right for you. But if you wanted to find a tech-savvy way to pinch pennies without noticing, automatic savings apps might just be a clever hack.

HIT UNSUBSCRIBE

Monthly subscriptions are sneaky little suckers. They lure you in with a free trial, then once you're on the hook, you're bleeding money each month for something you may not need or use. Ten dollars a month may not seem like much, but that's $120 a year. If you've signed up to multiple streaming services, subscription boxes, and magazines, then you could be kissing goodbye to thousands of dollars annually. So, do a subscription audit, remove all the ones you don't use enough to justify the cost, then divert that money straight into your savings account to grow your nest egg without even noticing.

HOW TO UNF*CK YOUR FINANCES · SAVING

HIDE YOUR MONEY

There's no need to stash your cash in a mattress like your great grandma did during the war. If you know you can't trust yourself to keep your mitts off your savings, then set up an account that can't be withdrawn from easily. Hiding money in a bank account that you can't get your paws on quickly is a great way to outsmart your spendthrift self. Some accounts can be locked, meaning you can't withdraw the money without going into a bank and signing a form (and often paying a penalty for withdrawal). These types of accounts stop temptation in its tracks as you won't be able to use that money for shopping sprees, YOLO-inspired trips to Bali, or everyday extras (like coffee and takeout food) that feel so damn good in the moment, but over time totally screw up your savings goals.

TRY THE 50/30/20 APPROACH

Knowing how much to spend and save is a minefield if you don't have healthy financial role models in your life. Applying the 50/30/20 method to your finances is a simple way to channel your money into the right places without studying economics. So, from your wages simply allocate:

50% toward essential living expenses such
as rent and utilities;
30% toward fun extras like new shoes,
make-up and pizza; and
20% toward savings and investments,
channeled into a separate account.

This method is a quick way to check if your lifestyle choices are within your financial means and if you're saving enough of your pay each month. If you're not saving much, start modifying those ratios and your bank account will soon start to fatten up.

BREAK IT DOWN

Want to save $5,000 by the end of the year? That amount might seem like an impossible dream until you break it down into bite-sized savings. To get there, you'll need to save $417 a month, which is $96.15 per week or $13.70 a day. Five grand now seems within reach, huh? This approach to saving will reframe how you spend money on discretionary items like takeout, snacks, movie tickets, and makeup. You'll never look at a $15 bottle of nail polish the same way again when $5,000 could be yours by the end of the year.

SAVE NOW, NOT LATER

Putting off saving money until you're older is tempting, but every year you delay saving will put you at a disadvantage later on. Compound interest is interest you earn *on top of* the interest you earn. It's a tricky concept to explain but American billionaire Warren Buffett credits his wealth to compound interest, so that should give you an idea of how potent it can be. The power of compounding is huge as your savings accelerate at a faster pace the longer you're in the savings game. So, the sooner you start saving, the more time you'll have to allow compound interest to do its thing. So, don't put off saving until you're older, save now and let compound interest do the heavy lifting.

AUDIT YOUR ACCOUNTS

Auditing your bank accounts will allow you to see where your money is going. If this is a scary thought, then you're exactly the type of person who will benefit from a deep dive into your spending patterns. So, roll up your sleeves, take a deep breath, and create a spreadsheet that tallies up and categorizes all your spending from the previous year. General categories like food, housing, clothing, transport, travel, and insurance are a good start. Sub-categories like coffee, takeout, and alcohol are also helpful if you're brave enough to go there.

As you audit your accounts, you may be shocked at what's revealed. Did you really spend $9,000 on clothes last year? Is your daily coffee costing you $2,190 per annum? This information (while confronting) will help you set your budget for the year ahead. It will show you where you're overspending and where you can cut back. Shining a light on your spending patterns is challenging but getting real about where your money is going is essential to budgeting. So get in there and flush those financial skeletons right out of your closet!

BUDGETING YOUR FINANCES HOW TO UNF*CK YOUR FINANCES

BUILD A BUDGET

It may sound like you're being asked to do homework, but it's going to be very hard to save money and assure your financial future without a weekly or monthly budget plan. Once you've got a handle on the amount you earn and spend, build a budget that accounts for every dollar you earn. Allocate your incoming cash to fixed-cost essentials first (like rent and car payments) then budget for everything else you spend money on in a month, accounting for food, transport, memberships, and more. This is now your blueprint for financial success. It's your choice to stick to it or not, but once you've created a budget you're officially on the path to glory.

USE APPS TO STAY ON TRACK

Setting a budget is only part of the equation, sticking to it is the other important piece of the puzzle. To ensure you're right on the money, use budgeting apps to check your progress regularly. Budgeting apps that are linked to your bank accounts take the grunt work out of keeping your budget on track. In the old days, people would keep every receipt and manually reconcile their own personal accounts to ensure they were within their budget. Now we have apps to do this for us! All you need to do is open your app and glance at how you're going to see if you can afford those new sneakers.

HOW TO BUDGETING TO UNF*CK YOUR FINANCES

BUDGET IN SOME FUN

Once you're set on saving money, budgeting can become an obsession. The problem with obsessions is that they tend to flame out early, leaving you back at square one. A good budget is one that you will stick to, so be sure to allocate some cash for having fun each month. Leaving some fat in your budget for things like movie nights and brunches with friends will ensure you don't feel too deprived while taking care of your finances. Using your money in joyful ways supports a balanced approach to saving. So, don't get carried away like Scrooge McDuck. Enjoy your hard-earned money responsibly, knowing that more will come your way.

BUDDY UP

Saving solo can be a lonely journey when all your friends are out blowing their pay at clubs and bars, so why not buddy up with another budgeter to walk the path together? Finding an accountability buddy to share your financial goals with is a great strategy to keep you in the zone when the going gets tough. Living on a budget can be problematic, especially during the early stages when you're trying to build new patterns and erase years of ingrained behavior. If you're struggling, find a likeminded friend who also wants to get their finances on track, and meet up once a month to share your wins, losses, victories, and fails. Exchange tips that have helped you budget, rage at the world when bills pile up and hype each other up when you hit your targets, because together you *will* make it happen.

BUDGETING
HOW TO UNF*CK YOUR FINANCES

WEED OUT REPEAT OFFENDERS

When building a budget, be sure to identify and kill off repeat offenders. These are the types of costs you see popping up on your bank statement over and over again but can easily live without. Common repeat offenders include eating out too often and relying on food delivery services instead of cooking meals at home, or using rideshare services to get around instead of walking or waiting for the bus. Over the course of a year, you could save thousands by cutting back on all these money drainers. When creating a budget for yourself, don't go cold turkey. Avoid making saving feel like a punishment by factoring in two coffees a week instead of seven and one meal out a fortnight instead of five. In time, you'll adjust to your new budget-friendly lifestyle and high-five yourself as your bank balance grows.

PLAN A PERFORMANCE REVIEW

Budgeting isn't a set-and-forget scenario. As your lifestyle, needs, goals, and earning power changes, so should your budget. Schedule in an afternoon each quarter to review your budget and make adjustments. If you've paid off your car loan or student debt (yes, it's possible) then tweak your budget to funnel that money into your savings or investments. If you've reached a savings target, modify your budget accordingly. Your budget should be a flexible plan that you review and adjust as your priorities shift. As you age you might go from saving your pennies for an overseas trip, to stashing cash for a new car, then building wealth to buy an apartment, and beyond. So, make sure your budget grows and changes with you, just like a healthy, supportive relationship should.

BUDGETING
HOW TO UNF*CK YOUR FINANCES

BUDGETING
HOW TO UNF*CK YOUR FINANCES

CHALLENGE YOURSELF

If you're a competitive person motivated by the glory of winning at all costs, then gamify the process by signing up for a budget challenge or creating one with your nearest and dearest. Okay, pitting friends and family against each other to see who can save the most money might not be for everyone, so consider signing up for an online budget challenge that will motivate you to keep your eyes on the prize. Budgets can be hard to stick to, especially when you have a hellish week at work and want to blow your cash on a margarita-fueled beach escape. A budget challenge will encourage you during the tough times and keep you on track to triumph, no matter what life throws at you.

BECOME YOUR OWN BOSS

If you're a motivated, hardworking, business-savvy bright spark with a killer idea, then becoming your own boss just might be your best bet. Although business ownership comes with risks and challenges, it also comes with unlimited earning potential. When you're working for someone else, there's a set salary threshold, but on your own? The sky's the limit. Whether you set up a nail salon, barber shop, or graphic design agency, you'll enjoy the freedom to set your own prices. You might be happy earning enough to live a comfortable life, or you may have dreams of setting up a multimillion-dollar enterprise. Either way, becoming your own boss frees you from the limits of earning what someone else thinks you're worth.

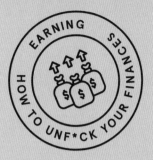

RAISE THE BAR

Asking for a raise can be daunting, but if you pull it off, it represents a relatively low-effort way to immediately boost your earnings. Many loyal, hardworking employees expect to be tapped on the shoulder by their boss and told they're getting a raise. Why not flip the script and ask your boss for a raise at your next evaluation? Lay out all that you bring to the table (skills, knowledge, education, passion, experience, hilarious banter) to show your value to the business. If your boss can't give you an immediate raise, they may budget in a raise for the next financial year. Sure, bosses can be intimidating, but you have nothing to lose by showing your worth as an employee. You could get thousands more dollars in your bank account each year because of one uncomfortable conversation, so stop sweating it, go forth and chase that raise.

STOP SELLING YOURSELF SHORT

If you're self-employed, listen up. One of the great advantages of being a freelancer is that you get to name your price. Whether you're an illustrator, videographer, or makeup artist, you deserve to be paid well for your time and skills. Underquoting is rife in most creative industries, so when quoting your prices, make sure your rate reflects your worth. If you haven't increased your rates in a while, up your prices to account for inflation. Many corporations try to undercut freelancers by offering low rates of pay. The next time someone tries to lowball you, stick to your guns and resist the temptation to lower your rate to suit their agenda. You have one... okay, two... agendas of your own: to do great work and get paid well for it. Now go out and command what you're worth.

HOW TO UNF*CK YOUR FINANCES · EARNING

START A SIDE HUSTLE

If cash flow is an issue and you don't mind using your spare time to generate extra moolah, then starting a side hustle can boost your bank account quick smart. Side hustles can be lo-fi (walking dogs, mowing lawns, cleaning cars), online (start a YouTube channel or Etsy store), crafty (create earrings or paintings to sell at markets) or a traditional business investment that has potential to grow into a full throttle money-making empire (think: food trucks, subscription services, fashion labels). Apart from generating cash, running a side hustle means you're less likely to spend your money to keep boredom at bay. Because when you're side hustling, you're way too busy to indulge in mindless online shopping or expensive concert tickets to see a band you're not even really that into.

KNOW YOUR RIGHTS AT WORK

So you've got a job? Awesome! But are you being paid what you're owed for your labor? Wage theft and underpayment is rampant, especially in retail and hospitality. So if you're busting your butt waiting tables, slinging cocktails, or flipping burgers, check that you're receiving every single dollar you're meant to. This varies from country to country, but if you're living somewhere that has a mandated minimum wage, make sure you're receiving it (or more). Check your pay slips to ensure that the hours and pay rate are correct, and if you're being short changed, raise it with your manager or union. It could be an honest mistake, or a dastardly plan hatched to boost profits while undercutting workers (thanks late-stage capitalism) but either way, you deserve to be paid every single cent that you're entitled to.

EARNING

HOW TO UNF*CK YOUR FINANCES

BECOME A PURVEYOR OF PERKS

From free lunchtime yoga classes to complimentary fruit in the lunchroom, many workplaces offer perks to staff. Don't be shy. Take advantage of all those extras and freebies. Work for a big corporation? Many corporate workplaces are invested in keeping their staff happy and healthy (so you're more productive, take fewer sick days, and are less likely to rage-quit). Take advantage of workplace health and wellbeing programs that offer discounted access to gyms, massages, and group fitness sessions. Many companies will also pay for education and training, so if upskilling on your boss's dime is a possibility, sign yourself up! Think of these perks as part of your salary package – it would be a shame to waste them.

EARNING

HOW TO UNF*CK YOUR FINANCES

LEVEL UP

If you've hit a brick wall in your career, it may be time to level up with more education. It's not a guarantee, but upskilling can increase your earnings if you're savvy about it. There's no need to go to college and study law though (although if you want to do that, go ahead). Instead, look into short courses and qualifications that will boost your earning capacity on the jobs market. Whether you're a vet nurse or chef, coder or engineer, continuous learning is key to career success and every dollar you invest in learning a new skill or getting a fresh qualification will help you command a bigger pay check.

TAP INTO THE SHARING ECONOMY

Passive income isn't just for landlords. The good news is that you don't have to be a property investor to generate rental income. If you've got a spare bedroom, car, garage, bike, parking space, or designer clothing and accessories, then you can boost your income by renting it out. If you don't use your car on the weekends, why not put it on an online car-sharing marketplace and make some extra cash? Have a spare room you never use? Get a roomie to reduce your housing costs. The sharing economy has opened up a ton of new ways for us to make money from our belongings, so put your stuff to work and reap the financial rewards.

BEWARE OF MLM SCHEMES

Got a friend who always tries to sell you essential oils? Keep receiving DMs from an old high school buddy who seems super enthusiastic about nutritional supplements? Chances are these people have been caught in the Multi-level Marketing (MLM) web. Often presented as a too-good-to-be-true, slick business opportunity that requires no qualifications, yet comes with free travel, conferences, and other perks, MLM schemes have exploded in the past few years.

Although they often seem like a great way to make easy money, dig a little deeper and you'll find many MLM schemes leave unsuspecting people financially worse off by getting them to sign up to buy large amounts of products they ultimately can't sell without using high-pressure tactics that end up alienating their friends, family, and co-workers. So before signing up to sell products for another business, check to see if the opportunity is right for you. If there are promises of financial freedom (that come with having to pay to be involved), then think again.

HAVE A FIRE SALE

Love sales? Instead of hitting the sales, try hosting one to make some coin while freeing up extra space in your place. Selling items you don't need or use is a liberating experience. Host a yard sale to offload homewares, list games and collectibles on eBay, and clear out your closet by selling your threads on Depop. If you have hoarding tendencies, set a reminder to hold an annual or biannual decluttering day, where anything you don't need gets sold. Collectively, billions of dollars of unused items are stashed in our homes. From dusty tennis racquets that haven't hit a ball in years, to brand new clothing with tags still attached, think of your belongings as dynamic items that can generate cash flow when you're done with them – not stagnant things that you don't use, but can't seem to part with.

BECOME A NEGOTIATOR

When you start a new job or accept a promotion, bottle your excitement for a second and train yourself to hold back accepting the salary you're first offered. While it's tempting to blurt out a hasty "yes" to a new role (especially if you've been unemployed for a while), asking your employer if they're open to negotiating the salary offer will signal your intention to earn more. This may be a highly uncomfortable conversation that goes against your natural instincts, but you could score a higher salary by having one simple discussion. If your salary can't be negotiated, then consider sounding out your boss about other potential perks like getting a phone plan paid for by the company. The art of the salary negotiation is one worth perfecting. You could instantly end up with thousands more in your pocket from one conversation.

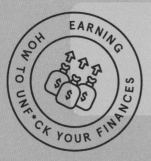

EARNING

HOW TO UNF*CK YOUR FINANCES

JOIN A UNION

From ensuring workers get paid vacation leave to making
workplaces safer, unions have fought hard to protect the rights
of workers and help hardworking people receive fair wages.
If you're lucky enough to live in a country where you have the
legal right to join a union, then signing up is a power move that
will help you and other workers to avoid exploitation now and in
the future. Negotiating wage rises is something that many unions
do on behalf of workers, so if you work in an industry where
unions have a good track record of pressuring corporations to
pay their employees fairly, then unite with your co-workers in
solidarity, join a union, and earn solid pay for your labor.

MONETIZE YOUR OPINION

Joining focus groups run by market research companies is
a nifty way to score some cash without putting in much effort.
From giving your opinion on car brands to talking about riveting
topics like toothpaste ads, focus groups reward everyday
people with cash or gift cards in exchange for an hour or so
of their time. Just say you get paid $100 per session and
you do four a year, that's an extra 400 bucks in your wallet for
only four hours' effort. Sure, you won't become a millionaire
from attending focus groups, but it's a nice little earner to help
boost your cash flow.

LOOK OUT FOR LIFESTYLE CREEP

Scoring a pay rise deserves a celebration, but don't let that party linger on for too long. Lifestyle creep is what happens when you start spending more as you begin to earn higher wages. A few special dinners here, a round of cocktails there, and soon enough your raise is gobbled up by lifestyle adjustments you unconsciously start making when your bank account is flush with extra cash. Instead, automatically funnel your higher earnings into clearing debts or boosting your savings and investments. Sure, treat yourself to a celebratory splurge on something nice, but be sure to adjust your savings or debt clearance rates as you increase your earnings too. Many high earners live pay check to pay check because they acquire a taste for the finer things in life. Don't become one of them when you start commanding coin in your career.

TRY MICRO-INVESTING

Not long ago, investing was something only rich folk could do. But thanks to micro-investing apps, anyone with a bank account and some cash can invest without having to pay a broker or come up with a hefty deposit. Micro-investing apps have leveled the playing field (to an extent), so that you can invest small amounts in the stock market here and there just by using your smartphone. You may believe that you don't have what it takes to be an investor, but the good news is that you don't need to be a Lamborghini-driving, Wall Street hotshot to make money from the stock market. School teachers, cleaners, carpenters, and librarians are all now investors thanks to micro-investing apps. So if you're curious about it, dip your toe in the market with a small amount to start your investing journey. May the stock market gods shower juicy gains on your micro-portfolio!

ADD ALTERNATIVE VENTURES

Not all investments need to be in cash or stocks.
The intersection between investing and hobbies is an interesting
one, especially if you find looking at financial statements or
stock market returns as fun as watching paint dry. If this is
the case, consider out-of-the-box investments such as art,
antiques, memorabilia, collectibles, or classic cars.
It helps if you're interested in any of these areas, as you'll have
a good eye for what items are likely to rise in value
over time. If you know what you're doing, a carefully curated
art, wine, or sneaker collection could yield big profits in
years to come. As with all investments, there's risk associated
with alternative investments, but if you're patient and take a
long-term approach to investing, that emerging artist
you bought a painting off could just fund your retirement in
30 years' time.

INVESTING
HOW TO UNF*CK YOUR FINANCES

CONSIDER CRYPTO

Not an option for sensible savers who steer clear of risk, cryptocurrency is a volatile (yet potentially highly lucrative) investment option that has shaken up the financial world. In 2009, Bitcoin emerged as the first decentralized cryptocurrency, but now there's a stack of different cryptos to choose from including Ethereum, Stellar, Nano, and Dogecoin, the cryptocurrency based on the Doge internet meme. Online trading platforms are the easiest way to dabble in crypto investing if you're a newbie. Just remember that you could lose it all or end up a millionaire – trading in the crypto scene is a pretty wild ride if you're game to saddle up.

PLAN FOR YOUR GOLDEN YEARS

The thought of getting older may terrify you, but you know what's more terrifying than wrinkles, silver hair, and hip replacements? Being old and broke. Whether you dream of becoming a golf-cart-riding Golden Girl in Florida or hope to live out your final years in an off-grid log cabin, the decisions you make now will either get you closer to or further away from your ultimate retirement scenario. Whatever your vision is for the future, having a retirement account is essential. If your workplace offers a retirement plan, be sure to make regular contributions. If you're self-employed, set up your own retirement account. Money might be tight, but every dollar you pump into the account will get you closer to living comfortably when you stop working. So save now, while you've got earning power.

ENLIST A ROBO-ADVISOR

Paying a human for financial advice can cost a bomb, but thankfully there's a low-cost way for newbies to access investment guidance without the high costs: robo-investing. Digital advisors (also known as robo-advisors) simplify the process for investors who want to put their money to work without doing all the research. Simply fill out an online questionnaire that will determine your risk profile, goals, and preferences. After you fund your account, your trusty robo-advisor will make investments on your behalf. Apart from hopping online to view your portfolio, you don't need to do much else except sit back and wait for your investments to grow.

INVEST IN YOURSELF

Sure, buying hot stock options is awesome, but your greatest asset will always be yourself. So when you think about investing, think about how spending money on yourself will pay off in the future. Investing in things like preventative healthcare, education, personal growth, and self-care practices will pay dividends in the future. Taking care of your health by keeping fit, getting regular health check-ups, eating a balanced diet, and acquiring skills and knowledge may lengthen your lifespan and boost your ability to earn money in the future. Every dollar you invest in your health and education will pay off in some way, either with increased earning potential or decreased healthcare costs later in life. Sadly, not everyone has access to good healthcare or education opportunities, but if you're in the fortunate position to make these investments in yourself now, it's one of the best places to channel your money.

HOW TO UNF*CK YOUR FINANCES · INVESTING

PUT YOUR GAINS TO WORK

If you've got dividend-paying stocks in your share portfolio, reinvesting any dividends or capital gains straight back into buying more stock is a common strategy to accelerate the growth of your wealth. If you're trading stock and make a nice profit or get a dividend paid out, it's tempting to take that gain and spend it on something fun. But by channeling it straight back into your portfolio, you'll compound your gains. Of course, there are risks associated with this. If you use a gain to buy a dud stock that sees its value dive straight after you buy in (yelp!), then you'll incur a loss. But if you're savvy about your stock choices, you'll see your portfolio's value grow at a faster rate than if you took your gains and blew it on a luxury watch you hoped would make you look like a baller. Instead, try reinvesting your gains and you'll be one step closer to being an *actual* baller when you're older.

FIND YOUR WHY

People invest for all types of reasons. Some want to be millionaires. Others want to enjoy a comfortable retirement. And then there are the people who want to support companies and industries that are aligned with their purpose. Reflecting on your reasons for investing will help you set (and hopefully reach) your investment goals. If your key reason for investing is to become a millionaire by 30, then an aggressive portfolio of high-risk stocks will be your go-to. If you're passionate about the environment and want to support wind farms, solar energy, or plant-based meat companies, then building your own portfolio of ethical stocks will be a better choice. So before you invest, think about what you stand for, what drives you, where you want to end up in the future, and how your money can help you get there.

GO SLOW AND STEADY

If your knowledge of the stock market is limited to what you learned while watching *The Wolf of Wall Street*, then put your investing on easy mode by placing your money in ETFs (exchange traded funds) and index funds. These types of investment products take the stress out of having to choose high-performing stocks yourself. A low-effort way to spread your money across a diverse range of shares, index funds, and ETFs pool money from investors and use that money to invest in a variety of stocks and bonds. Instead of having to research different stocks, these types of funds do the legwork for you and are considered lower risk than choosing individual stocks. Sure, you probably won't see your profits go to the moon like Reddit investors chasing meme stock gains, but over time, it's highly likely you'll accumulate a healthy return to enjoy in your golden years.

SPREAD YOUR RISK

Putting all your money on black is fun on a Las Vegas roulette table (if you win), but when it comes to investing, spreading your risk is a winning (yet less exciting) strategy that has made many investors super wealthy. Diversification is key to a healthy, stress-free investment portfolio that delivers solid returns in the long run. This is why investing in high-risk stocks or dicey get rich quick schemes is a bad idea. You may end up a winner, but the high exposure to risk also means you could end up bankrupt. So diversify your investments by spreading the risk across cash, property, retirement accounts, alternative investments, and a variety of shares in different companies. If you're new to investing, you may not be ready for property, but the method is still the same – don't put all your eggs in one basket!

INVESTING

HOW TO UNF*CK YOUR FINANCES

TRY FRACTIONAL PROPERTY INVESTING

If buying a whole house or apartment is out of your reach, fractional shares in property might be right for you. Fractional property investment allows multiple unrelated people to invest in property by buying a percentage share in commercial or residential buildings. Once the domain of cashed-up moguls, property investing is easier and more accessible than ever before thanks to online platforms. You won't be able to live in the property, but you'll have an investment vehicle to carry you forward into the future.

GET INTO SOME WHISKY BUSINESS

Some of the best investment choices can come from left field and putting your cash into a barrel of whisky is one of those wild ideas that has paid off for some investors. Recently, the value of rare whisky has taken off in a big way, with some bottles of Scotch whisky selling for more than a million bucks at auction. Whisky investment companies have opened up ownership to the average person by offering cask ownership and storage via online platforms. You won't get an instant return though, as whisky appreciates over time, with decades needed to see profits. Currently, the global demand for this aged spirit is outstripping supply, so the return on investment is predicted to be high. So, if you like the idea of becoming a whisky millionaire, join the aged-spirit investment scene.

CASH YOURSELF UP

Credit and debit cards are convenient, but they have a dark underbelly: they cause you to spend more money than you have. Handing over cash hits differently than swiping plastic, and that's why studies have shown that people who pay with cold, hard cash end up spending less than card users. While retailers are encouraging you to swipe your card and tap your phone instead of reaching into your wallet, buck the trend and choose to pay for everything with cash. It will make you more accountable and odds are, you'll end up spending less.

SCOUT OUT STUDENT DISCOUNTS

Studying can be a real hard slog, but at least it comes with student discounts. From accessing a cheap cell phone plan, to buying discounted movie tickets and shopping at stores on special "student days," there are benefits to being a student. The key to maximizing these benefits is to be incredibly strategic about where and when you spend your dough. Plan your dates around student discounts – if Tuesday night is student night at your local pizzeria, then make that a standing date with your friends. Get in the habit of asking stores if they offer a student discount – many don't advertise their deals very well. Don't be shy, tap into those savings while you can, because when you're older, you'll sorely miss your student discount privileges.

SPENDING

HOW TO UNF*CK YOUR FINANCES

INVEST IN MEMBERSHIPS

If you love visiting museums, galleries, or theme parks, it makes good financial sense to buy a membership or annual pass. While the upfront cost may look a little daunting, memberships are a great buy when you factor in the cost of each visit. Many schemes also offer perks like preview nights with complimentary drinks and snacks. Yes, you heard right – free snacks. But remember, annual passes and memberships are only financially beneficial if you use them – so schedule lots of visits into your diary to squeeze every last bit of value out of the deal.

HOW TO UNF*CK YOUR FINANCES · SPENDING

GET SWAPPING

Save money on your grocery bill by making a few simple food swaps. Drink tap water (if safe) instead of buying bottled water. Substitute rolled oats for more expensive steel-cut oats. Use boneless chicken thighs instead of more costly chicken breasts. Make bolognese using lentils instead of meat. Use your blender to make homemade oat milk instead of buying the packaged version. Buy block cheese instead of shredded cheese. Pop your own popcorn instead of buying a pre-popped bag. You could save hundreds (or more) over the course of a year just by swapping ingredients here and there. You won't really notice the difference in your meals, but you'll notice it in your bank account!

SPENDING

HOW TO UNF*CK YOUR FINANCES

BULK UP

It almost always works out cheaper to buy larger quantities of food and common everyday items. While this sucks for single people who live alone and don't want a huge bag of rice haunting their pantry for a year, with a little meal prepping and menu planning, bulk items can be used to your financial advantage. Sure, if you're on a budget, it's tempting to buy the smallest (and cheapest) option on the shelf, but if you compare the price per gram or pound, you'll find the smaller sizes to be the most expensive. Better still, hit the stores that specialize in selling bulk foods to stock up on large quantities of nutritious ingredients like oats, lentils, beans, rice, nuts, and canned tomatoes. You'll need to play a little pantry Tetris to squeeze them all in, but your bank balance will be healthier for it.

CHOOSE ITEMS WITH STAYING POWER

Before you buy certain items, ask yourself: "Is it built to last?" In the short-term, buying the cheapest option on the rack might seem smart, but if that cheap brand breaks or wears out in a week or a month, then it's not actually cheap – it's a rip off. If you invest in a good pair of shoes, a well-made leather belt, or a top-quality set of knives, you could have these items for years – potentially decades – before they need replacing. So before buying anything, look beyond the price tag (which isn't a good indicator of value). Think about the item's potential lifecycle and whether you'll be paying to replace it in six months or still using it when you're old and gray.

PLAY THE WAITING GAME

Hands up if you're accustomed to that crummy feeling of buying something on impulse, then not feeling so great about it when you get home? If you're lucky, unused items can be returned at some stores, but there's a way to avoid this scenario altogether. Simply set yourself a challenge to wait 48 hours before buying anything other than essentials. This tactic will give you time to assess if you *really* need that winter coat (when you already have three coats in your wardrobe). By taking the emotions out of seeing something you just "have to have," you can better establish the difference between a need and a want. Two days later, you probably will have forgotten about the coat altogether, will have an extra $200 in your bank account and won't have to feel guilty about buying something you end up wearing twice before donating to a thrift store years later.

HOW TO UNF*CK YOUR FINANCES

SPENDING

EMBRACE THE SECONDHAND ECONOMY

In case you hadn't heard, our planet is drowning in stuff. From yard sales to online marketplaces, you can buy almost anything secondhand for a fraction of the price you'd pay in stores. Need some fresh threads for your new job? Thrift stores are full of lightly worn affordable fashion. Want to furnish your apartment on a budget? Online marketplaces are filled with listings for cheap beds and couches. Have blank walls to fill in your room? Unique, vintage oil paintings can be picked up at yard sales or flea markets for a steal. Every time you buy something secondhand, you'll be saving money and reducing the amount of junk that ends up in landfill. The only thing to remember with used items is there won't be warranty provided, so if you're risk averse, steer clear of buying secondhand big-ticket items like televisions or laptops. Otherwise, go forth and save your pennies (and the planet) by buying preloved items.

SHOP SEASONALLY

Timing is everything when it comes to bagging a bargain. When shopping for food, it's cheaper to buy fresh fruit and vegetables when they're in season. Winter typically welcomes a glut of potatoes, beets, and citrus fruits, while summer is the season of low-cost tomatoes, peaches, pineapples, and cherries. So, get your fill when they're ripe and you'll not only save money, they'll taste better too! On the other end of the spectrum, shopping out of season is smart when you're buying clothing or holiday items. Savvy shoppers buy their Christmas decorations in January, winter coats in spring and bikinis in early autumn when stores slash prices to clear stock. Follow this formula and you're guaranteed to save money all year round.

SPENDING · HOW TO UNF*CK YOUR FINANCES

FIND FREE EVENTS

Live music is costly if you're accustomed to spending money on tickets to concerts and festivals. Don't deprive yourself of live events – just find the free ones. Orchestras and music companies put on free concerts, bars have frequent acoustic sets that don't require a ticket, pubs have free open-mic nights, and local governments often put on free concerts for the community to mark holidays and cultural celebrations. If you're itching to find something fun to do, check online for free events in your area before parting with any cash.

BE AN
EARLY BIRD

If you like to travel, you'd be familiar with the concept of dynamic pricing. Airfares, hotels, and long-distance rail tickets are usually priced dynamically, meaning that the cost of a ticket changes dependent on availability of seats and rooms. Many people hold out for last-minute deals but buying well in advance is often a solid way to secure a cheaper rate. So, if you want to save money on your adventures, get in the habit of planning and booking your breaks months ahead of time. Sure, you might like to indulge in spontaneous breaks, but if you're booking an airfare or hotel room the day before you leave, the chances are you'll be paying a premium, especially if you're traveling on weekends or during holidays when prices surge like an Uber fare on New Year's Eve.

SPENDING

HOW TO UNF*CK YOUR FINANCES

SALE

40%

CRACK THE CODE

Before you buy anything online, check to see if you can apply a promo or discount code to save yourself some cash. From shoes to makeup, hotel stays, and more, promo codes can save you a chunk of money if you use them consistently. Saving $5 here, 10% there and accessing free shipping is a simple way to save without putting in much effort. Simply search promo codes online, check the brand's social media pages for codes, or download one of the many apps and browser extensions that automatically scan and apply any available discount codes to your cart before paying. Just say you spend $1,000 online each year and you use promo codes to access 10% discounts on each transaction, you'll get an extra $100 in your pocket without even trying.

= $00.00

40%

SWITCH LABELS

From prescription drugs to canned beans, generic labels are a cheaper option that many people don't consider for a range of reasons. There's a perception that generics are poor quality, but many generic labeled goods are made in the same factory as the more expensive, premium items. Generic labels are also subject to the same laws as other brands, so stores can't legally sell items that are unsafe for consumption. Ultimately, if you want to save on your grocery and drugstore bills, then substituting for generic labels is the easiest, quickest shortcut to savings town. Simply make the switch and save.

HOW TO UNF*CK YOUR FINANCES · SPENDING

JOIN A CO-OP

Food cooperatives are grocery businesses that are owned and run by members. A great place to source organic and bulk produce with minimal packaging, food co-ops typically support small brands, organic growers, and local farmers over the big corporate giants. Apart from sticking it to the supermarket chains, joining a food co-op can help you save money on your grocery bills. When you buy seasonal produce in bulk, you'll pay less. When you buy products without packaging, you'll also usually pay less because you're bringing your own containers instead of paying for manufactured, single-use plastic bottles, lids, labels, and bags. Some food co-ops offer member discounts or free produce if you volunteer your time to help run the store. If there's a co-op in your area that you've dismissed as being a hippie hangout, think again. Food co-ops will help you save money (and lighten the load on the planet).

PREPAY AND SAVE

Many insurance companies offer discounts for coughing up an annual fee instead of paying in monthly instalments. If you think it seems unfair that people who can't afford to pay upfront are being penalized, then you'd be right. But if you're fortunate enough to have enough money to pay your car insurance annually, then choose that option to save a chunk of cash. Some hotels also offer discounted rates for prepaying for your room before you arrive – a great option if you don't intend to cancel or change your travel dates. It might feel counterintuitive to lock away your money in advance, but in the long run, you'll spend more if you don't.

GET INTO COUPONING

Anyone who has ever watched TLC's reality series *Extreme Couponing* knows that coupons can shrink your grocery bill if you play your cards (or is that coupons?) right. Not everywhere in the world has a strong coupon culture, but if you're lucky enough to live somewhere where coupons proliferate, then it's your duty to make the most of the scene. Before you go to the supermarket, find coupons that align with your needs. Using coupons to stock up on bulk amounts of essentials is wise. After all, you can never have too much peanut butter in your pantry. You can find free printable coupons on coupon websites, on product packaging, in store catalogs, or within grocery store apps if you prefer to go digital. You may only save a few dollars each shopping trip, but over the course of a year, that will add up to some serious savings (and a stockpile of goodies you got for a steal).

SPENDING · HOW TO UNF*CK YOUR FINANCES

PRIORITIZE EFFICIENCY

Bagging a bargain is exciting, but what if that steal ends up costing you more in the long run? If you're buying a new fridge, washing machine, clothes dryer, or dishwasher, the one with the cheapest price tag might not be the cheapest after all. Say what? Energy and water efficient appliances may cost a little more upfront, but over their life cycle they'll end up saving you money on water and power bills. Just say your dishwasher lasts 12 years and you run it once a day – that dishwasher will end up clocking more than 4,000 cycles over its lifetime. That's 4,000 opportunities to use less power and water, making a big dent in the amount you fork out on bills. With household appliances like fridges, freezers, washers, and dryers accounting for an estimated one-third of our household energy bills, choosing efficient models over cheap brands is a winning strategy for your wallet.

MASTER MEAL PLANNING

Before heading to the supermarket, sit down and hit peak adulting levels by planning what meals you'll make in the week ahead. Meal planning is a simple way to save money on food as you'll be less likely to waste ingredients if your fridge is stocked with items that you'll definitely use in recipes you're planning to make. If you know you're making pumpkin soup, a pasta bake, burritos, cobb salad, and meatloaf over the course of the week, then these are the only ingredients you'll need to buy. Armed with your trusty shopping list, you'll stay on track instead of wandering the aisles in a fog of confusion, grabbing random ingredients that end up going to waste. Take this idea one step further by batch-cooking a stack of freezer-friendly meals made with in-season, inexpensive vegetables. With a freezer full of tasty as hell home cooking, you won't need to drop cash on drive-thru burgers on the way home from a long day at work, because you've already got better options at home.

PLAY THE EQUATION GAME

Sometimes, you just need to shock yourself out of spending money. So, before you buy anything, equate the cost to the number of hours you'd have to work to get it. If you earn $15 an hour, then that $150 dress will cost you 10 hours of labor. Want to take that trip overseas that costs $5,000? That journey will cost you a whopping 333 hours of work on a $15-an-hour wage. Of course, this method doesn't factor in taxes and bonuses, but what it does do is change your mindset. You'll never look at spending money in quite the same way ever again – and that's a good thing.

HOW TO UNF*CK YOUR FINANCES · SPENDING

REFINANCE YOUR STUDENT LOAN

If you're like most people, you'll leave college with a bunch of new friends, a brain full of knowledge, and unfortunately, a stack of student debt. This experience of being indebted so young can be incredibly depressing, so many people avoid looking at their student loans altogether. The problem with avoidance is that the issue is still there, humming away, unchanged, potentially getting worse each passing day. Instead of avoiding thinking about your student loans, channel your energy into finding a better deal. By refinancing your student loans you can save thousands each year on interest and cut the life of your loan by years. So assess your student loan account regularly, refinance with a lower interest rate, and you'll achieve freedom from your evil student loan overlords in good time.

TRY THE SNOWBALL METHOD

Paying off multiple debts but feel like you're getting nowhere? Debt can be soul destroying if you let it linger for too long, so look at everything you owe (credit cards, personal loans, car payments) and find the smallest debt among the bunch. That's the one you want to hit hard and pay down first. Once that debt has been kicked to the curb, channel your payments into the next smallest debt. This strategy, known as the snowball method, provides great incentive to become debt-free, because you can celebrate wins along the way by killing off debts one by one. The boost in confidence and momentum that comes from clearing that first sucker will carry you forward to take down all your other financial liabilities too.

HOW TO UNF*CK YOUR FINANCES

DEBT BUSTING

CONSOLIDATE YOUR DEBTS

Got multiple credit cards and personal loans hanging over your head? It can be mighty hard to keep up with payments when you've got so many debts accruing interest each month. Debt consolidation will bundle up all your debts into one neat package that attracts a lower interest rate. This method will reduce your total debt from "scary" to "less scary" and organize it into one simple, stress-free monthly payment, which of course you'll make each month, right?

TRANSFER YOUR BALANCE

Is credit card debt getting you down? Soul-crushingly high interest rates can make it feel like you're going backwards when you're trying to pay down debt. Transferring your balance to a credit card with an introductory 0% interest rate is a good strategy to help you whittle down your credit card debt. With a long, merciful break from paying interest, you'll be able to make a big dent in the amount you owe without pesky interest adding to the burden. Of course, the key is to not make purchases on your card, otherwise you'll only add to your problems. So, if you're stuck in a never-ending cycle of making credit card payments, do a balance transfer to another card with an interest-free introductory offer to send that credit demon straight to hell, right where it belongs.

DEBT BUSTING · HOW TO UNF*CK YOUR FINANCES

GO BEYOND THE BARE MINIMUM

Making minimum payments on your credit card is a sure-fire way to stay in debt for a long, long time. Just say you buy a $2,000 laptop on your credit card and make the minimum repayments. Depending on the interest rate, if you only make the minimum monthly payments, you could end up paying for that laptop for 15-plus years. You'll also pay about triple the ticketed cost. By that time, your laptop will be dead and buried and you'll still be paying for it! Free yourself from the minimum-payment trap by paying above and beyond the suggested amount each month.

BUCK THE BUY NOW, PAY LATER TREND

Buy now, pay later services are fast emerging as one of the most popular payment methods on the scene, but they're not without risk. These platforms can be handy to get you out of a tight spot when you need to buy something essential before payday. But if you're in the habit of using these services to fund shopping sprees, then you're setting yourself up for future financial failure. This way of spending just kicks the can down the road for future you to deal with. It might seem appealing to spread the cost of a new pair of sneakers across several weeks but what these platforms do is encourage low-income earners to spend more than they can comfortably afford. Just like credit cards, ensure that you don't overcommit to spending amounts of money you'll struggle to pay back.

DEBT BUSTING

HOW TO UNF*CK YOUR FINANCES

PROTECT YOURSELF FROM "STDS"

You may know how to protect yourself from HPV, but there's another STD you need to be aware of: Sexually Transmitted Debt. Falling in love is a wonderful feeling, so wonderful that we can make decisions that aren't in our best interests. In the early stages of romance your hormones run wild, so it's easy to see the object of your affection through rose-colored glasses. This is where things can get tricky (and costly). If your lover is asking to borrow money, co-sign on a car loan, or become an authorized user on your credit card, think long and hard before agreeing. Because when the thrill is gone, you may end up saddled with their debt. It's an expensive lesson to learn, but one that you can avoid if you're strong enough to set boundaries and protect your credit, at all costs.

LIVING

HOW TO UNF*CK YOUR FINANCES

SLAY YOUR BILLS

PAID

While it's tempting to pretend your phone bill doesn't exist or that parking ticket was just a bad dream, it's better to accept it and pay up – pronto. Late payment fees add up, and every time you put off paying bills, you're wrecking your credit score. If you're in the habit of paying your bills late for no good reason, then wise up and slay those suckers as soon as you get them. By doing this you'll save money on late payment fees, keep your credit score healthy and relieve the mental load associated with having your electricity cut off or debt collection agencies hounding you. If you genuinely can't pay a bill on time, call the company to negotiate a payment plan or get an extension. Either way, addressing the situation almost always leads to a better outcome than burying your head in the sand and hoping the bill will magically disappear (because sadly, we all know it won't).

PAID PAID

READ CONTRACTS

Whether you're buying a gym membership or signing a rental car agreement, be sure to read the contract before signing on the dotted line. Don't skim it, scan it, or speed read it. Make a coffee, sit down and read every single word so you understand how this contract will impact your finances. Is there a costly exit fee? Are there sneaky add-ons or extra charges? How long is the agreement for? Does the contract auto-renew each year? If anything doesn't sit right, don't sign it. And if you're not sure about the language, get a trusted, in-the-know friend to look at it for you. Too many people have been burned by getting stuck in costly scenarios that are near-impossible to get out of, so before you sign anything, know what you're getting yourself into.

TIME YOUR TRAVEL

Nothing compares to the sheer joy of blowing off all responsibilities to jet off somewhere far, far away from your workplace or school. If you're keen to slash your travel budget, try traveling in the off-season. Prices always heat up in the peak travel seasons, so avoid holiday periods and save. Hotel rooms come at a premium on the weekends, so try a mid-week break to snap up a luxe room at a fraction of the cost. Beachside destinations are popular during summer, but they're also overrun with crowds. Try an autumn break by the ocean to have the beach to yourself while saving money at the same time. With a little thought and planning, you could save big bucks by traveling when everyone else isn't.

DOWNSIZE, MINIMIZE, ECONOMIZE

Consumerism has a lot to answer for. Our lives are littered with costly things we don't need or use. Kitchen gadgets you use once a year, dusty gym equipment that lies dormant in your garage, clothes that don't fit – our homes are haunted by hasty purchasing decisions of years gone by. The pressure to keep adding more and more stuff to our lives is huge as we're constantly bombarded with advertising persuading us that happiness can be found in a new novelty sweatshirt. Downsizing your life doesn't mean you have to live in a cave and wear sweaters hand-knitted from recycled cat fur. Take steps toward minimalism by auditing your life. Do you really need a car? Can you rely on a bike or public transport instead? Is your home too big for your needs? Can you move somewhere smaller that's cheaper to heat, cool and maintain? Make a commitment to only buy new things when an item reaches the end of its life cycle. So instead of upgrading your phone every six months, use it until it dies (then recycle it). The minimalist approach takes some getting used to, but you'll soon discover the financial (and personal) freedom that comes with having less.

BECOME A MAINTENANCE EXPERT

Taking care of your valuables is one of those unsexy, overlooked ways to save money that your parents probably lecture you about while your eyes glaze over. Getting your car serviced regularly, cleaning your air-con filters frequently, removing the lint out of your clothes dryer often, and not overloading your washing machine are all simply ways to extend the life of your appliances. It may also help them to run more efficiently, resulting in lower electricity and gas bills. Items like cars and washing machines aren't cheap to replace, so treat them with care and you'll get years more wear out of them (and give your parents a reason to smile).

GET HELP

Do you have trouble with gambling? Are you drowning in credit card debt and don't know how to get out? Do you rely on payday loans to get by? When money becomes a huge source of stress, bring in the big guns to help you out. Financial counseling can help you get to the bottom of the money issues that are impacting your ability to live a comfortable, secure life. Experts in financial counseling will be able to provide solidarity and sound advice. They'll hook you up with organizations and services designed to help people with financial challenges. It may feel a little overwhelming, but once you've got a plan in place and someone on your side to help you, you'll feel lighter and more empowered to work toward a brighter future. You got this!

KICK BAD HABITS TO THE CURB

Everyone knows the health risks associated with smoking, drinking, and gorging on fast food, but there's a financial cost too. Cigarettes, alcohol, and double cheeseburgers with a side of loaded fries have little-to-no nutritional value yet are expensive when you make a habit of indulging in them. If you've ever thought about quitting smoking, becoming a teetotaler, or cutting back on your fast food habit, then consider the financial gains you'll make when you channel the money you spend on smokes, vodka, and burgers straight into your savings account? In 10 years' time you'll have tens of thousands of extra bucks and a healthier bod too. Quitting vices isn't easy, so use your finances to motivate you to triumph over temptation.

LOVE YOUR LOCAL LIBRARY

If you're a book lover and want to save money, then it's a no brainer to join a library. If you haven't set foot in a library since your youth, then prepare to have your mind blown about what contemporary public libraries offer. Far from being stale, musty environments policed by overzealous seniors in cardigans, modern libraries are vibrant, dynamic community spaces brimming with life and energy. Your library card will unlock access to so much more than free books. You can borrow everything from cake pans, to magazines, toys, tools, and DVDs. Your membership will also give you free access to online databases and courses, music and movie streaming services, and eBooks. Libraries also host free events like author talks and book clubs. Thanks to free Wi-Fi, good lighting and lots of power outlets, many people now also use libraries as free co-sharing spaces. Is there anything libraries can't do?

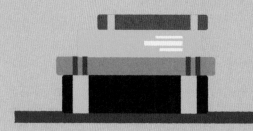

BE SURE TO INSURE

Buying insurance is one of those annoying purchases that many of us tend to resent because seemingly you get nothing in exchange for paying your annual premium. But you know what's worse than paying for insurance? Not having it when you need it. Renters insurance will shield you from the costs associated with theft or damage when your upstairs neighbor floods their bath, sending cascades of water through your ceiling straight down onto your leather couch, flatscreen TV and vintage rug. Insuring high-value items like your engagement ring, brand new mountain bike, or collection of rare vinyl records is wise because the one-off cost to replace these items will be hard to wear. It's sad to imagine your favorite items being stolen or damaged, but it's a fact of life that these things happen. Do you have enough money in your bank account to replace the contents of your home? If not, get insurance so you're not left holding the bag through no fault of your own.

LIVING
HOW TO UNF*CK YOUR FINANCES

BECOME A DIY GURU

So many goods and services we buy out of convenience and a lack of understanding about just how damn easy it is to do it yourself. Beauty products like exfoliants can easily be made at home using dirt-cheap ingredients like oil, brown sugar, oats, or coffee grounds. Don't spend money on expensive chemical cleaners when you can make your own cleaning products with inexpensive ingredients like white vinegar, water, lemon juice and baking soda. Don your overalls and watch some YouTube tutorials to learn how to complete minor house repairs (we're talking changing showerheads, not fixing electrical faults) instead of paying professionals. You'll still need to buy the materials, but labor costs are usually the bulk of what you pay for basic home repairs. Plus, the smug satisfaction that comes with successfully pulling off a DIY project comes for free.

LIVING · HOW TO UNF*CK YOUR FINANCES

CULTIVATE A KILLER CREDIT SCORE

If you live in a country where people live and die by their credit scores, then it's in your best interest to build and protect yours. Even if credit scores aren't such a big thing where you live, your credit rating will still have an impact on your life in some way. Easy ways to protect your credit score include not defaulting on loans, paying all your bills on time and never missing monthly credit card payments. Having a credit card with a small limit that you pay off every single time is one strategy people use to cultivate a good credit rating. Building credit isn't a fast process, as financial institutions want to see proof that you can manage money over time. It may seem like a pointless exercise when you're younger but having a healthy credit score will unlock lower interest rates and give you a better chance at getting approved for car loans. In many ways, your credit score has the potential to make or break your future, so build good credit from the get-go and your life will not only be easier, it'll cost you less too.

GET WITH THE PROGRAM

Rewards programs and loyalty clubs are well worth signing up to, especially if you're a brand-loyal type of person. If you fly often, then earning airline miles toward making your next flight a free one is a no brainer. Same with hotels and rental cars that allow you to accrue points every time you make a booking. Beyond redeeming your points for free flights or hotel stays, you'll often get access to fancy executive lounges stocked with complimentary drinks and snacks so you don't have to spend $15 on a sad, stale airport bagel.

LIVING · HOW TO UNF*CK YOUR FINANCES

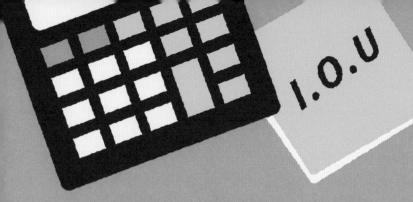

SPLIT BILLS THE SMART WAY

Getting together for dinner with a group of friends is fun, until the bill comes. Who has cash? Who ordered the lobster? How big a tip should we leave? Inevitably, one person ends up paying on their credit card, then chasing the rest of the group to cough up what they owe. If you're the type of person who avoids confrontation, you'll often end up wearing the cost of the filet mignon that a guy called Ryan ordered before conveniently dropping off the face of the earth, leaving your bank account looking anemic. Apps like Splitwise help you to bypass the awkwardness associated with hunting down your friends (or frenemies) to pay their fair share. Beyond dinners, apps like Splitwise can help you divvy up other shared expenses like household groceries and utilities bills without having to leave passive aggressive notes for your roommates.

WEED OUT FINANCIAL FRENEMIES

Unbalanced relationships are a source of many financial problems, especially when one person gives without getting much back. Got a friend who expects you to pay for their dinner all the time? What about a family member who always borrows money (but never pays it back)? Or a roommate who never chips in to pay for groceries? While it's admirable to help friends and family when you can, if your relationship doesn't have genuine reciprocity, then perhaps it's time to address the situation and stop mooches from draining your finances. Setting healthy boundaries can be difficult, but any true friend would understand that you're a human being, not an ATM.

JOIN THE FIRE MOVEMENT

Do you dream of flipping your desk, storming out of work and never coming back? Retiring at a young age is the ultimate end game for many of us, but how are you going to get there? The FIRE (Financial Independence, Retire Early) movement advocates for young people to go extremely hard and fast with their earnings, savings, and investments. This movement is all about having multiple income streams, including at least one that will generate passive recurring income in the future (i.e. an online business or a large investment portfolio). To get there, you need to save and invest heavily in your 20s, 30s, and 40s – a difficult thing for most people as they establish themselves in their careers while paying off student debt. People living the FIRE lifestyle tend to be high earners, so there's an amount of privilege required to channel a large percentage of your earnings into savings and investments. But if you're working in a high-income profession and aspire to retire early, then the FIRE method might get you there.

BECOME A FREEBIE FINDER

Before buying anything for your home, keep an eye on your local Freecycle networks. These online communities offer veritable goldmines of goodies you can have for nix. From beds to washing machines, dining tables and sports gear, Freecycle networks are a great way to furnish your home or replace items without parting with a cent. Sure, the items will be secondhand, but often people offload good-quality, working appliances and homewares when they're moving home, upgrading, or renovating. So, adopt the "best things in life are free" mantra and get down with freecycling.

RUN YOUR OWN RACE

They say that comparison is the thief of joy, and this is never truer than when comparing your financial situation with others. Keeping up with the Joneses is a sure-fire way to end up broke or in massive amounts of debt. If you can't work out how your friend can afford to own a luxury car, go on overseas trips, and wear designer threads, then relax in the knowledge that they are either: a) in extreme amounts of debt, b) being spoilt by rich family members, or c) a drug dealer. A good approach to finances involves living within your means and making sound financial decisions based on the resources you've got at your disposal. Some people will always have more than you, others will have less – but none of that concerns you because you're running your own race, right?

FACE YOUR DEMONS

Many of our attitudes toward money are shaped in our infancy. Just as you inherited your father's brown eyes, you can also inherit his crappy attitudes toward money. Never underestimate the impacts of seeing a parent go bankrupt or use retail therapy to fill the gap in their heart left by a brutal divorce. The messages you receive during childhood can impact your self-esteem and world view, but they can also affect your ability to earn and save. If you're prone to undervaluing yourself, overspending, over giving, or making risky money moves that don't pay off, consider unpacking how your family views money. If you see a therapist, bring it up as a topic you'd like to explore, because there's no point setting a budget you'll never stick to if you haven't excavated the real reasons why your relationship with money is beset with issues. Facing your money demons is tough work – you may need to undo decades of programming. But the insights you receive will change the game for good.

FIND A MONEY MENTOR

You may already see a career mentor or life coach, but do you talk about money? Money mentors can offer valuable guidance and ideas that will flip your thinking. Unlike financial planners, money mentors won't provide specific strategies about where to save or invest. Instead, they'll unearth how you feel about money and provide inspiration to help you reach your goals. If you want to earn more in your career, they'll suggest ways to help you get there. If you're running a business, a money mentor could help you brainstorm ways to increase cash flow. Whether you pay for a professional money mentor or lean on a trusted family friend known for their financial wizardry, a money mentor will help you bring home the bacon.

BOOST YOUR FINANCIAL LITERACY

In high school you were no doubt forced to study trigonometry, but how much did you learn about money management? While you can now calculate triangle angles with ease, how are your finances going? Most high school curriculums have a gaping hole where financial literacy should be, but don't let that stop you learning about money later in life. Listen to financial podcasts, read blogs full of money-saving tips, and borrow books on budgeting from the library – do everything you can to get up to speed on all things money. You don't need to become an overnight expert or get an economics degree; you just need to be knowledgeable enough to know what terms like "compound interest" mean and how they have the power to change the course of your whole damn life. No biggie.

LOWER YOUR CREDIT LIMIT

When you apply for a credit card, your bank will assign you a credit limit, but there's no reason why you must accept or keep that limit in place. If you're prone to overspending and can see your debt spiraling, call your bank to lower your credit limit to a modest amount. Credit cards can be helpful in emergencies and can also assist you to build a credit score, so set a small limit on your card to stop budget blowouts and other self-destructive acts of spontaneous spending.

HOW TO UNF*CK YOUR FINANCES · LIVING

STAGE A FEE FIGHTBACK

From credit card annual fees to monthly bank fees, many financial institutions charge their customers reoccurring fees. But what many people don't know is that these charges are often waived with one simple phone call. If you're being charged fees that you don't want to pay, call your bank to tell them you're unhappy with the fees and would like to close your account. Often, banks will waive the fee to keep you as a customer. Financial institutions rely on the compliance and apathy of their customers to rake in millions each year. So, stage a fight back and free yourself from fees.

LIVING
HOW TO UNF*CK YOUR FINANCES

GET OUT OF TOWN

It can be incredibly hard to get ahead financially if you live on a modest wage in a High Cost of Living (HCL) area. If you're living in a city that appears high on the Cost of Living Index, then you're probably paying a pretty penny to rent a sub-standard apartment. So, consider making a move to a more affordable area. While this approach won't work for everyone, if you can move to an area where rent, utilities, and food are cheaper, then you could save thousands each year. Even better if you can keep your current job and work remotely from a more affordable city or town. Moving won't be worth it if you'll miss your family too much or have to leave your career behind, but if you've lost that loving feeling with your overpriced city, then maybe a breakup will free you to explore your options in more budget-friendly places.

BE A MORNING PERSON

Spending time with your buddies is non-negotiable, but the time you often catch up isn't. If you're accustomed to pulling all-nighters with your friends, then you'll be familiar with that dreadful feeling that comes with checking your bank account the morning after a big night out. Drinks, followed by dinner, followed by more drinks can cost hundreds of dollars just for one night of fun (soon followed by days of regret). So simply swap your social time to the morning for a more budget-friendly catch-up session. Grab a coffee and bagel for $10 or meet at the park for a run followed by a smoothie. Unless you're meeting in Vegas, morning catchups are less likely to involve expensive meals and costly cocktails. So, make AM dates with your besties a thing and reserve your nights for quiet, cost-free nights in.

BECOME A BILL DETECTIVE

If you're a fan of true crime and love the idea of catching culprits in your spare time, then put that energy to work in your own life by inspecting your bills and financial statements. Allocate some time each month to comb through your statements looking for discrepancies. Did the nail salon double charge you for that manicure? Is the yoga studio still charging you for a membership you canceled six months ago? Why did that $17 lunch magically turn into a $170 charge on your card? Mistakes are made all the time and retailers rely on consumers to be lazy or naive to get away with overcharging. So get in the habit of checking your statements to weed out financial crimes in your own backyard.

MAKE A MONEY MOOD BOARD

Looking for a fun creative project to get stuck into during your next crafternoon? Gather up all your old magazines and make a money mood (or vision) board to help you stay focused on your journey to financial freedom. Some cynics write-off vision boards as woo-woo garbage, but setting intentions is a powerful way to distill your goals into one neat package while enjoying getting your craft on. What's not to like? Whether you choose to decorate your board with pictures of luxury homes or inspiring words that drip with abundance, a vision board is a colorful reminder of why you're saving, investing, and budgeting. Want to keep your eye on the prize? Create a money mood board and display it somewhere you'll see it every day.

GO FOR GRANTS

LIVING · UNF*CK YOUR FINANCES

Got a great idea that will improve your community?
Hoping to study a course but can't afford it? Want to
travel to a conference but don't have the funds to
make it happen? Many philanthropic organizations offer
grants and sponsorships to help dreams come true.
From building a community garden, to studying dance
in New York, or starting a small social enterprise
that helps the homeless, grants and scholarships are
well worth applying for if you're big on ideas but low
on liquid assets.

GIVE YOURSELF AN ALLOWANCE

Sure, you're an adult now, but there's no reason why you can't give yourself an allowance each payday. Many of us grew up receiving a weekly allowance from our parents, so keeping this habit up shouldn't be so hard. Each payday, give yourself a set amount to spend and do not go over it unless there's an emergency expenditure like an urgent car repair. Withdrawing a set amount of cash to use for the week is a good way to keep yourself honest and accountable. The rest of your wage then gets funneled into investments, savings, or debt reduction. By staying within your set allowance, you'll naturally adjust your lifestyle to live within – not beyond – your means.

PAY IT FORWARD

If you're excelling at unf*cking your finances then congratulate yourself with a metaphorical ticker tape parade. Once you're done fist pumping the air and basking in the glory of financial freedom, take a minute to think about others who aren't in your position. Using your money to help lift others out of poverty is one of the most impactful ways to honor your journey. Ending up in a privileged financial position comes with responsibility to your community. Sure, you could just keep your hard-earned cash to yourself, but sharing with people who need it the most elevates society to a better place. Every dollar you give to schools, food banks, homeless shelters, and funds that support underprivileged people to succeed in life, is a dollar well spent. So when you can, share your abundance with others and help someone else unf*ck their finances too.

Smith Street Books

Published in 2022 by Smith Street Books
Naarm | Melbourne | Australia
smithstreetbooks.com

ISBN: 978-1-92241-763-3

Publisher: Paul McNally
Editor: Kate Symons
Design and illustration: George Saad

Printed & bound in China by C&C Offset Printing Co., Ltd.

Book 201
10 9 8 7 6 5 4 3 2

MIX
Paper from
responsible sources
FSC® C008047